GET READY FOR PENTASCALE DUETS!

by Wynn-Anne Rossi and Victoria McArthur

PENTASCALE DUETS

Check Off (✓) when completed successfully with duet

INSTRUCTIONAL ACTIVITY PAGES

Pachelbel in C

Secondo

Johann Pachelbel (1653-1706, Germany)
Adapted by W. Rossi

Theme from **Canon in D**

Pachelbel in C

Primo

Vivaldi in G

Secondo

Antonio Vivaldi (1678-1741, Italy)
Adapted by W. Rossi

Theme from **Spring** (*The Four Seasons*)

Vivaldi in G

Primo

Bach in D

Secondo

Johann Sebastian Bach (1685-1750, Germany)
Adapted by W. Rossi

Theme from **Sheep May Safely Graze**

Bach in D

Primo

Handel in A

Secondo

George Frideric Handel (1685-1759, Germany)
Adapted by W. Rossi

Theme from **Hallelujah Chorus** *(The Messiah)*

Handel in A

Primo

Mozart in E

Secondo

Wolfgang Amadeus Mozart (1756-1791, Austria)
Adapted by W. Rossi

Themes from **Eine Kleine Nachtmusik** and **Sonata in C, K.545**

Mozart in E

Primo

Beethoven in B

Secondo

Ludwig van Beethoven (1770-1827, Germany)
Adapted by W. Rossi

Themes from **Ode to Joy** and the **"Moonlight" Sonata**

Beethoven in B

Primo

Rossi in F♯

Secondo

Wynn-Anne Rossi (b. 1956, U.S.A.)
Adapted by W. Rossi

Theme from **Giant Purple Butterflies** *(Trip Through the Rainforest*)*

*Published by The FJH Music Company Inc.

Rossi in F♯

Primo

Chopin in F

Secondo

Frédéric Chopin (1810-1849, Poland)
Adapted by W. Rossi

Theme from **Fantaisie-Impromptu, Op. 66**

Chopin in F

Primo

Brahms in B♭

Secondo

Johannes Brahms (1833-1897, Germany)
Adapted by W. Rossi

Theme from **Lullaby** (from *Five Songs*, Op.49)

Brahms in B♭

Primo

Tchaikovsky in E♭

Secondo

Peter Ilyich Tchaikovsky (1840-1893, Russia)
Adapted by W. Rossi

Theme from **The Nutcracker, Op. 71**

Tchaikovsky in E♭

Primo

Joplin in A♭

Secondo

Scott Joplin (1868-1909, U.S.A.)
Adapted by W. Rossi

Theme from **The Entertainer**

Joplin in A♭ 

Primo

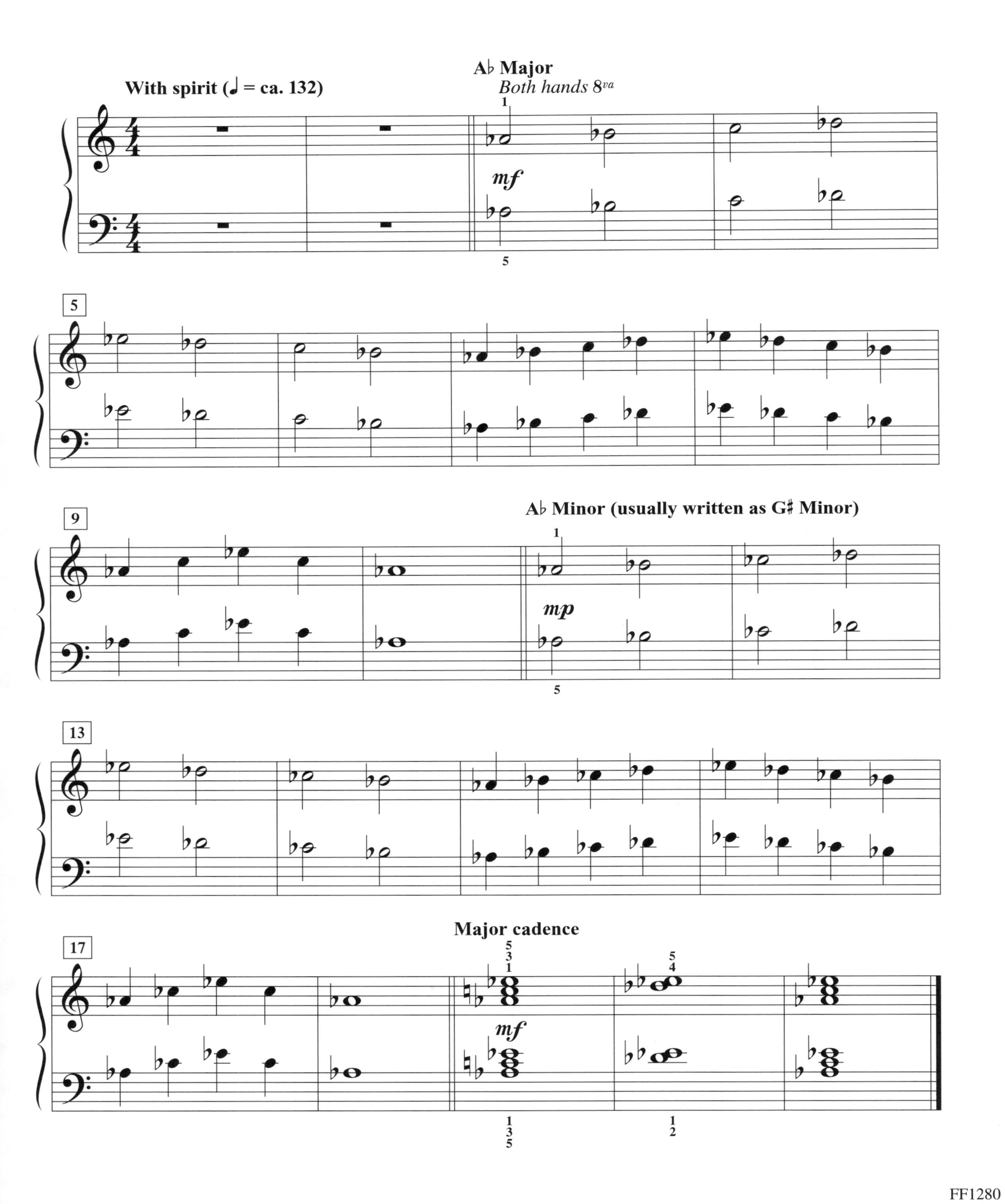

Stravinsky in D♭

Secondo

Igor Stravinsky (1882-1971, Russia; U.S.A.)
Adapted by W. Rossi

Theme from **The Firebird**

Stravinsky in D♭

Primo

Fishing for Facts About Pentascales

Pentascales

All pentascales have **five** notes.
Each note is a step (2nd) apart.

Some pentascales use all white keys.
Some pentascales need some black keys.
These are written using **sharps** ♯ and **flats** ♭.

Major Pentascales

To create the major sound, there must be a half step between notes **3** and **4**. All the other notes are a whole step apart.

The step pattern is **W W H W**.

E Major pentascale

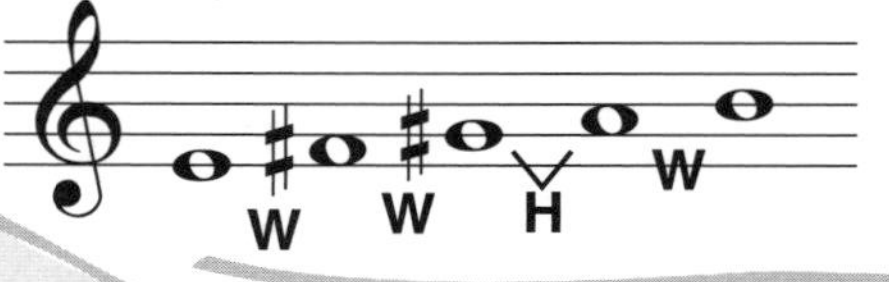

Minor Pentascales

To create the minor sound, there must be a half step between notes **2** and **3**. All the other notes are a whole step apart.

The step pattern is **W H W W**.

The easiest way to create minor from major is to **lower** your third finger one half step.

C Minor pentascale

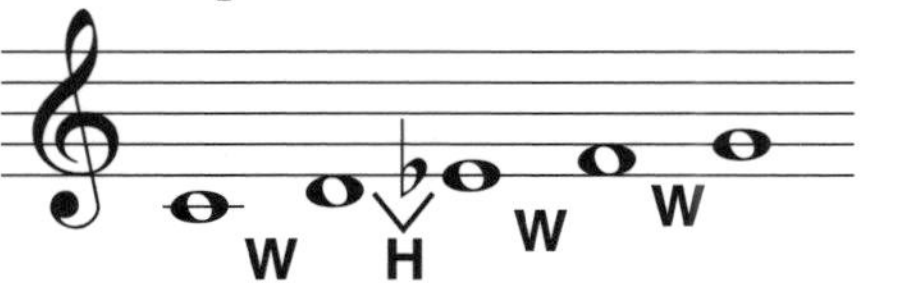

Hidden Treasure!

Penta-secret: **Listen** carefully whenever you play a pentascale to decide if it sounds major or minor. Remember the step pattern.

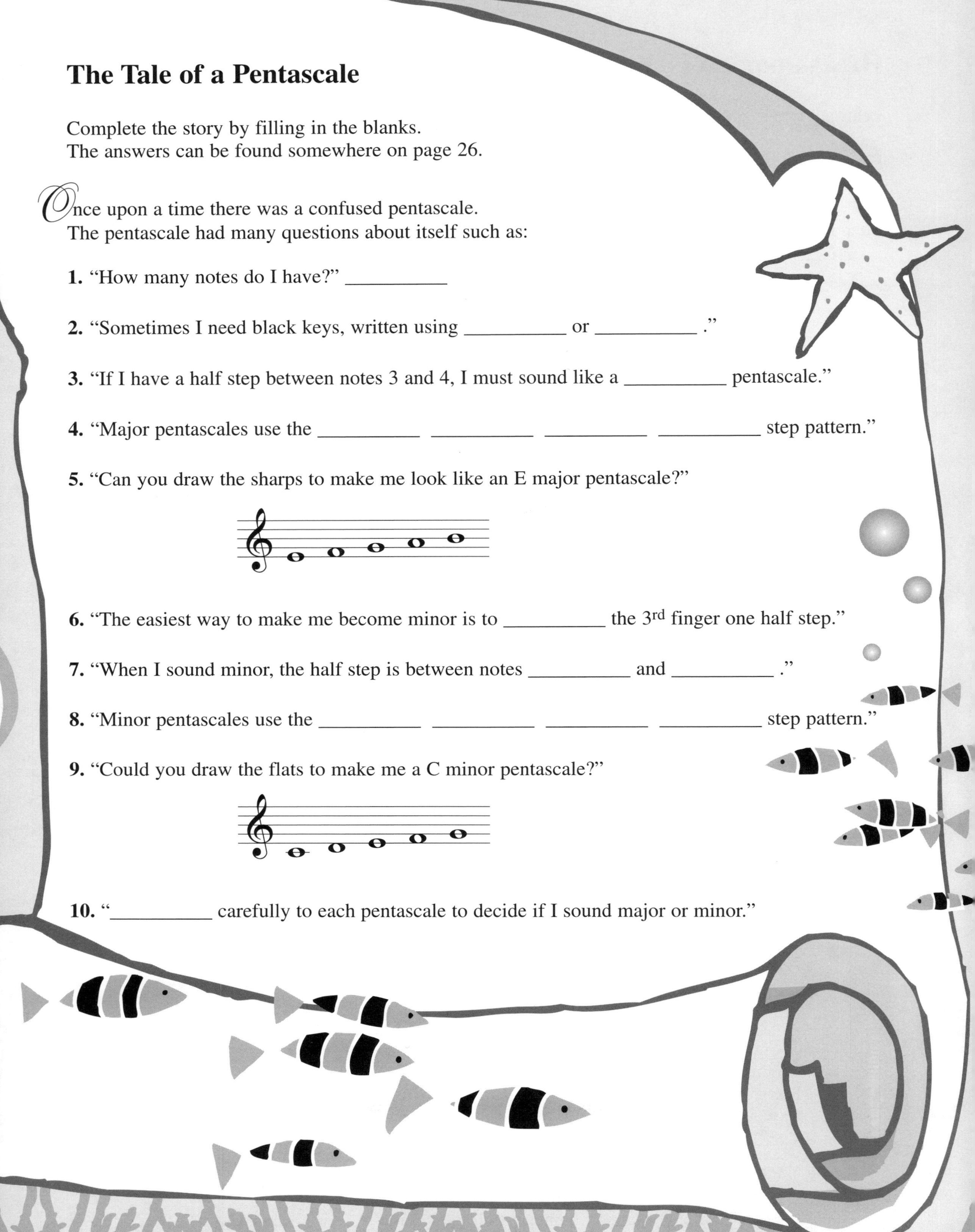

The Tale of a Pentascale

Complete the story by filling in the blanks.
The answers can be found somewhere on page 26.

Once upon a time there was a confused pentascale.
The pentascale had many questions about itself such as:

1. "How many notes do I have?" __________

2. "Sometimes I need black keys, written using __________ or __________ ."

3. "If I have a half step between notes 3 and 4, I must sound like a __________ pentascale."

4. "Major pentascales use the __________ __________ __________ __________ step pattern."

5. "Can you draw the sharps to make me look like an E major pentascale?"

6. "The easiest way to make me become minor is to __________ the 3rd finger one half step."

7. "When I sound minor, the half step is between notes __________ and __________ ."

8. "Minor pentascales use the __________ __________ __________ __________ step pattern."

9. "Could you draw the flats to make me a C minor pentascale?"

10. "__________ carefully to each pentascale to decide if I sound major or minor."

Great Composers' Book Corner

Learn about the great composers in this book.

First correct the spelling of each name.
Mark through the wrong letter. Write the name correctly above.

Then read the **Fun Notes!** about the composer's life.

Fun Notes!

Pachelbel
♪ *Johann Nachelbel* (*see page 2*)
The Pachelbel Canon became very popular again over 250 years after it was written.
It was the theme music for the 1980 award-winning movie, *Ordinary People*.

♪ *Antonio Vivalvi* (*see page 4*)
Sometimes he was called "The Red Priest" because he wore red priest's robes and had thick curly red hair.

♪ *Johann Sebastian Back* (*see page 6*)
This famous German composer wrote over 1,200 musical pieces.
He had 20 children, 5 of whom were named Johann.

♪ *George Frideric Vandel* (*see page 8*)
When Handel's most famous piece called *The Messiah* was first performed, King George of England stood in surprise when he heard *The Hallelujah Chorus*. Since then, people stand as a tradition.

♪ *Wolfgang Amadeus Mozatt* (*see page 10*)
Mozart loved animals. He liked to eat liver and dumplings. To play all of Mozart's music, it would take about 200 hours (almost 10 days and nights in a row).

♪ *Ludwig van Baethoven* (*see page 12*)
Macaroni and cheese was this famous composer's favorite food.
He never paid attention to whether his clothes were clean or his hair was combed.

♪ *Wynn-Anne Bossi* (*see page 14*)
She is currently one of Minnesota's happiest composers. She celebrates life by writing music in the morning, taking walks by Lake Minnetonka with her dog, Max, and rollerblading or cross-country skiing in the park.

♪ *Frédéric Choppin* (*see page 16*)
He was called the "poet of the piano." For a practical joke, he enjoyed putting people to sleep with soft playing and then waking them up with a bang.

♪ *Johannes Brahma* (*see page 18*)
At the first performance of his *First Symphony*, only a few people clapped. Brahms had many friends but he never married. This is probably good since he snored loudly.

♪ *Peter Ilyich Tthaikovsky* (*see page 20*)
His famous *Nutcracker Suite* is one of the most recorded pieces in classical music. Tchaikovsky gave away half of the money he made and spent the rest on nice clothes, expensive food, and other things for himself.

♪ *Scott Jotlin* (*see page 22*)
He was America's most famous African-American composer. He is called the "Father of Ragtime Music." His favorite book was *Alice's Adventures in Wonderland*.

♪ *Igor Strabinsky* (*see page 24*)
He once said that "my music is best understood by children and animals."
He wrote a polka that was performed by 50 animated elephants wearing ballet tutus.

Review Game

THE MERRY PENTA-GO-ROUND!

A fanciful ride on the backs of major (or minor) animals.

Directions: Ride every animal on the Penta-Go-Round.
As your teacher points to an animal, play the pentascale.

Note to Teacher: You may ask the student to play either major or minor.

Pentascale Practice Flashcards

(to add variety to practice)

Student Directions:
Cut out the flashcards by following the dotted lines. Then shuffle them. Draw one from the stack and follow the practice directions on the flashcard. Use pentascales you have been assigned or other pentascales of your choice.

CUT HERE

Play *legato* and *forte (f)*.	**Play *staccato* and *piano (p)*.**
Play your right hand *forte (f)*, and your left hand *piano (p)*.	**Play your right hand *piano (p)*, and your left hand *forte (f)*.**
Make your pentascale sound: excited, sleepy, angry (choose one)	**(teacher's choice)**
Make your pentascale sound: lazy, busy, happy (choose one)	**(your choice)**

CUT HERE

Play *staccato* and *piano (p)*.

Play *legato* and *forte (f)*.

Play your right hand *piano (p)*,
and your left hand *forte (f)*.

Play your right hand *forte (f)*,
and your left hand *piano (p)*.

(teacher's choice)

Make your pentascale sound:
excited, sleepy, angry
(choose one)

(your choice)

Make your pentascale sound:
lazy, busy, happy
(choose one)